WHY SAY NO TO SEX

Why Say No to Sex?

The case for teaching sexual abstinence outside marriage

JOSH McDOWELL

Edited by John and Janet Houghton

KINGSWAY PUBLICATIONS

EASTBOURNE

ISBN 0 85476 525 5

Produced by Bookprint Creative Services
P.O. Box 827, BN21 3YJ, England, for
KINGSWAY PUBLICATIONS LTD
Lottbridge Drove, Eastbourne, E Sussex BN23 6NT.
Printed in Great Britain.

Contents

Editors' Foreword

Josh McDowell is one of the most popular speakers alive today. In the last twenty-three years, in the course of 18,000 talks, he has addressed over eight million students and teachers in universities and secondary schools spanning seventy-two nations. He is the author of over thirty best-selling books and has featured in numerous films and videos.

A graduate in economics and business, with degrees in languages and theology, he also holds honorary doctorates in law, theology and literature.

Concerned about the tragic consequences of teenage sexual promiscuity in the Western world and the failure of so-called 'value-free' sex education to address the issues effectively, Josh McDowell argues cogently for a restatement of the values of chastity, fidelity and personal responsibility in sexual behaviour among unmarried teenagers.

This book comprises extracts from *The Myths Of Sex Education* adapted for the British reader, which we present as a resource tool for parents, youth workers teachers and school governors who are prepared to challenge the status quo and to offer our teenagers the option of sexual dignity and self-worth. It is a message urgently needed in an age of disillusionment, AIDS, family breakdown and rising sexual violence.

John & Janet Houghton
(Authors of *Parenting Teenagers* and *A Touch of Love*)

1
The Quest For Intimacy

'Mr McDowell, in the last five nights I've gone to bed with five different men.'

The young university woman was speaking to me over the phone from several hundred miles away. 'Tonight,' she said, 'I got out of bed and asked myself, "Is this all there is?"' Then she began crying. When she regained her composure enough to speak, she said, 'Please tell me there's something more.'

'There certainly is,' I said. 'It's called intimacy.'

We face a teenage sexuality crisis today. Yet our main problem is not sexual, it's relational. We have embarked on a fruitless quest for intimacy without understanding what real intimacy is. We have allowed our culture to convince us that the only way to find intimacy is through physical involvement.

I am personally convinced that most young people use sex in an attempt to find intimacy. They don't want sex as much as they want closeness with another human being. Yet they have been duped by the statistics into believing that sexual involvement is what they want most. That's not true. When you dig a little deeper, you discover that kids don't want to be sexually involved as much as they want to be loved. They want someone who really cares for them. A sixteen-year-old girl wrote to me after my last tour of England: 'Josh, I want someone to love me. Not physically—I want someone who cares. I want to love and be loved, and I don't know how to do either.'

Today we see young people getting involved in sexual activity— often promiscuous sexual activity—for the simple reason that they don't understand what true intimacy is. Sexual experience becomes a substitute for intimacy. We use phrases like 'making love' and 'being intimate' in talking about sexual intercourse. Yet most sexual involvements outside the loving commitment of marriage express very little genuine love or closeness.

Young people today want close, caring relationships and mistakenly think that saying yes to sex means saying yes to intimacy.

This false understanding has caused untold damage in our society and has blighted the lives of thousands of teenagers. Yet, in spite of the overwhelming evidence to the contrary, 'value-free' sex education, with its blithe promises of 'safe sex', continues to sustain the myth that personal fulfilment is to be found in sexual experimentation outside the bounds of marriage.

I believe there is a better way. I believe it is to be found in abstinence-based sex education.

2
Contrasting Views

There are two basic views of sex education. The traditional view says that sex education is for the purpose of preparing young people to enjoy to the maximum the marvellous gift of sex within the context of marriage and for the benefit of society as a whole. In contrast, those who promote morally neutral sex education believe that young people primarily need to be trained to use contraceptives and make choices. Comprehensive, or 'value-free', sex education is seen as a means of reducing the number of unwanted teenage pregnancies and slowing the spread of sexually transmitted diseases.

Behind these two diverse purposes are radically different moral presuppositions. Advocates of value-free, morally neutral sex education see man as the product of a long evolutionary process. He is a sexual animal who is not necessarily monogamous or heterosexual. Sex has no meaning beyond pleasure and the propagation of the species. There is no reason to exercise control over one's sexual behaviour. In fact, any restriction or prohibition of sexual behaviour is seen as likely to be harmful.

Compare the so-called morally neutral view to the Judeo-Christian world view which sees man as created in the image of God with dignity, worth and potential. Sex is an expression of love, not the satisfaction of lust. Man has the ability to make moral choices and control his sexual behaviour. Within the commitment of a monogamous marriage relationship, sexual intercourse is a beautiful and profoundly meaningful act—a vital form of interpersonal communion between two persons who are uniquely different and yet complementary to each other.

Because of the supreme value placed upon marriage and the family in this view, premarital and extramarital sex must be prohibited. Furthermore, the exploitation or perversion of any sexual relationship is not only counterproductive, but degrading and damaging to anyone involved. According to this view, some forms of sexual behaviour are very right, while other forms are very wrong.

One of the most basic and crucial differences between the views of those people advocating the 'value-free' education model and those advocating the abstinence model concerns the human versus animal contrast.

The *value-free* sex education model promotes the 'philosophical view of man as just a higher animal (B.F. Skinner . . . Pavlov, etc.). He can't stop biological urges. . . . All one can hope for is to provide training (contraceptives) and a way out for mistakes (abortion).'

The *abstinence* model sees man as having a mind, intellect and spirit, a rational being who can exercise self-discipline, think abstractly and make decisions based on future expectations. People have the capacity to dream, to choose and to love.

We're not talking about animal sexuality; we're talking about human sexuality. We're talking about young people created in the image of God with personal dignity, respect for themselves and others, and the capacity to say no and abide by it. We're talking about teenagers who, given the opportunity and encouragement, can make right moral choices and carry them out. The moment we surrender this truth about our kids, we put them in the same category as dogs in heat. It is realistic to expect our kids to wait. Our kids are not animals. They can control their hormones and their desires.

3
The Myth Exposed

In the past twenty-five years it has become generally accepted that any teaching about sex in the state schools should be free of moral judgements. 'A moralistic education,' says Sol Gordon, 'seeks to influence children to accept a particular religious or idiosyncratic point of view.'[1] According to many people, the present generation has no business imposing its views on the next generation. We're told that our kids have minds of their own and must be allowed to use them. The teacher must act only as a neutral catalyst for discussion to help students discover their own values.

It has become moralistic, and therefore unacceptable, to tell students that certain sexual activities are wrong while others are right. 'We must be value-free and morally neutral and let students make their own choices.' 'Sex education should present all the options for sexual expression without explicity encouraging or discouraging teenager sexual activity.' A former US Secretary of Education Bennett summarises this position (which he opposes): 'While students are told it is okay to say no to sex, they are not told they ought to say no.'[2]

Perhaps the greatest deception perpetrated on the parents of teenagers in this country is the myth of value-free, morally neutral sex education. I have never met anyone, let alone a teacher, who can act as a neutral catalyst on any subject, let alone sex. Whenever a kid is around an adult, the adult's values will be communicated either verbally or nonverbally.

Anne Marie Morgan, formerly an educator and psychology teacher and now a parent, observes:

Despite its claims of being 'neutral', comprehensive sex-education is not truly value-free. Listing certain options gives value to them, with the endorsement of the authority of the state and the school behind those options. If, for example, a parent has taught his child that abortion is wrong, and the school says that it is not, but merely one of many opinions, this undermines the parent's attempt at inculcating that value.[3]

It's not a question of whether or not sex education teaches values or morals: it's a question of whose values and which moral code is best or right. The claim that comprehensive sex education is value-free and morally neutral is a myth.

Barrett Mosbacker observes:

It is philosophically and intellectually impossible to be morally neutral. To claim either actively or passively that there are no moral absolutes is to embrace moral relativism and situational ethics. This is a moral frame of reference. Either sexual activity is presented as having moral parameters, or as having no parameters, but both are equally moral statements.[4]

Obviously, the Judeo-Christian view of sexuality is not morally neutral, but then it doesn't claim to be. Those who claim moral neutrality, on the other hand, are in fact hiding behind a clever facade which 'gives the impression of being neutral and objective. . . . As they write and as they teach, their moral—or immoral—presuppositions or assumptions will come through.'[5]

What so many sex educators overlook today is that sex is a social act involving at least two people. As a social act, the way partners treat each other is not determined by the physical or biological aspect of sex: how the penis enters the vagina, how a condom is rolled on, etc. Rather the relationship is determined by the character of the individuals. And character is based on values. We dare not teach sex to young people without teaching character, and we cannot teach character without teaching values. If we surrender the responsibility for developing morality, values and character to our children alone, then we must be ready for the devastating physical and social consequences they will suffer.

I do not believe that 'morally neutral education' can ever provide an adequate basis for saying no to premarital sex. It certainly does nothing to build a young person's understanding of the concepts of family or character. Sex education without traditional values is not only pointless, but it is also harmful to young minds.

4
Abstinence Is Positive

At this point, it must be kept in mind that effective abstinence-based programmes don't begin and end with 'Just say no!' There's more to abstinence education than that. The 'just say no' campaign wouldn't be very effective in dealing with the adolescent sexual crisis if all we did was say to kids, 'Don't do it!'

The 'pill and condom' advocates seem to ridicule and mock the 'just say no' stance as being naive and out of touch—fantasising. One example is a statement by free-lance writer Beverly Walth, in the *Dallas Times Herald*: 'Sexual abstinence is a fantasy solution.' She states emphatically that advocates of abstinence 'put forth the view that the solution to the problem of teenage sex is merely to tell them not to do it.' Walth continues, 'What irritates me most about this manner of thinking—if there is any thought buried in there at all—is that abstinence is a fantasy solution to these very real problems.'

Please realise that neither I nor other abstinence education advocates are endorsing or promoting a simplistic 'just say no' approach to the teenage sexual crisis.

Dr Dinah Richard, who consults with American schools on abstinence-based sex education programmes, defines it positively:

It teachers that human behaviour, including the sex drive, is controllable and that the sex act itself is a beautiful expression of love properly occurring between a husband and wife. Besides the unitive role of sex, the procreative aspect within a marriage is presented as an exciting event that brings forth new life. Abstinence education helps teenagers realise that sex in the wrong context will result in unfortunate consequences. By stressing avoidance, teenagers can enjoy greater freedoms in their present and future lives.

Abstinence education is factual sexuality instruction placed within a moral context. It covers information about human anatomy and development, pressures to be sexually active, consequences of sexual activity, resisting the pressures to become involved in sex, freedoms that accompany abstinence, building positive freindships, appropriate dating behaviours, resolving conflict, communication with parents, future plans, marriage, parenting and family life. It covers many of the same topics found in other sex education courses, but differs in the direction the teacher leads the students and the perspective it offers on the issues.[6]

A good example of positive abstinence sex-education in the United States is the Sex Respect course.

The Sex Respect course provides ample material to fill ten hours of classroom time covering the following topics.

Aspects of human sexuality

The programme stresses that human sexuality is much more than biological. The subject of sexuality is treated respectfully and with dignity. Students are shown how to respect others, themselves and their own sexuality.

Parents who are concerned that their children's privacy and innocence will be offended in a sex education course are assured that the Sex Respect programme seeks to protect the modesty of teenagers. For example, biological information is presented as a quick review of material already learned in science classes rather than being emphasised as the most important aspect of sex. Students are directed back to their parents for discussion about topics that are more controversial or sensitive such as masturbation, homosexuality and abortion. The programme recognises that parents are the experts in determining the level of understanding, sensitivity and maturity of their own child and guiding the discussion accordingly.

Mature love and sex

Instead of telling teenagers that premarital sex is OK as long as the couple love each other, Sex Respect tells teenagers that they must be mature in every respect—not just the physical—before they can handle a sexual relationship. The programme emphasises that it is only in the life-long commitment of marriage that sexual intercourse can bring fulfilment. Outside marriage, sex has many negative emotional, psychological, physical, social and spiritual effects which can cause serious and often irreversible harm. Teenagers are also told that unless they are ready for fidelity and commitment in marriage, they aren't ready for parenthood. And if they aren't ready for parenthood, they aren't ready for sex.

How to say no to sex

Clear directions are given to help teenagers 'just say no' to premarital sex. For example, the Sex Respect text lists ways to build self-confidence and assertiveness and provides an exercise that challenges students to think up effective responses to 'chat up lines' they might hear from members of the opposite sex. They are also shown how their speech, actions and personal appearance can say no to sex, and how a host of little decisions made during the course of a date can either lead towards or away from sexual activity. For example, a choice to drink on a date may weaken a teenager's resolve and lead to later sexual activity. A decision not to watch a sexually explicit movie on a date may keep a couple from getting aroused and involved.

Students are taught that sex doesn't 'just happen'. It is the result of a number of little decisions made along the way. Throughout the Sex Respect course teenagers are challenged to think about the choices they will confront and plan their dates carefully instead of drifting aimlessly into sexual situations. Sex Respect emphasises specific information about how to avoid the many pressures to engage in premarital sex that young people face.

Secondary virginity

For teenagers who are already sexually active, the course introduces the concept of 'secondary virginity': the decision to stop premarital sexual activity. Sex Respect challenges students by reminding them that they are human, not animal, and humans have the ability to reason and to choose. A teenager is capable of deciding not to engage in premarital sex at all. Even those teenagers who have made some poor decisions about their sexual behaviour in the past can decide to practice abstinence in the future. Teenagers are advised that practising secondary virginity is not easy, but that it is possible and tremendously rewarding.

A sexually active female undergraduate, whose unmarried mother was also promiscuous, confided in the health education teacher after the chapter on secondary virginity, 'I never knew I could say no'. Sex Respect helps teenagers realise they have the power to say no whether or not their virginity is intact, or whether or not they have positive sexual role models.

Other topics covered in the Sex Respect course are sexual freedom versus sexual impulsiveness, consequences of teenage sexual activity, and dating guidelines.

Throughout the text, students are challenged to think seriously about the issues of human sexuality and to respond in ways which help them make the concepts and language their own.

Another strong quality of the Sex Respect programme is that it taps into the idealism of youth. Many teenagers are aware of sex-related mistakes made by their parents, older siblings and peers, and they want something better for themselves. A number of these young people recognise that they should wait until marriage to become sexually active. They are looking for adults who will tell them that abstinence is the best choice and that it is possible to save sex for marriage.

For example, one exercise appeals to teenagers' idealism by asking, 'What are some of your goals for the next ten years?' and 'How might involvement in premarital sex prevent you from realising these goals?' The chapter on parenthood explains that a healthy marriage is the ideal environment for raising children and points out the negative impact on children when they lack loving, caring parents—a situation which many teenagers have experienced themselves and wish to avoid when they have children of their own. Sex Respect is designed to bring out the best in teenagers and to give them higher moral standards to reach for.

Where this strategy is being implemented in schools and youth clubs a remarkable reduction is taking place in the crisis areas of teenage pregnancies, abortion and the incidence of sexually transmitted diseases. Something positive can be done!

Teens respond positively to Sex Respect's message that sex is good, not bad, when experienced in the right context.

Early chapters explain that sexual intercourse is meant to express a union on the mental, social, emotional and spiritual levels as well as the physical. When the sexual union involves all these dimensions, both partners experience the fulfilment of their human need to love and to be loved. Idealistic teenagers are hungry to hear that their sexuality takes on its deepest meaning and offers its greatest fulfilment within marriage and that married sex is well worth waiting for.

Abstinence makes a lot of sense to a lot of teenagers. In a study conducted in the junior high schools of a major US city, 67 percent of the kids said their greatest need in sex education was learning how to say no to sexual pressure. So many give in to sexual pressure when they don't want to be involved sexually. It requires strong personal integrity to be able to resist someone you like and possibly love. Personal integrity is needed to make decisions that are compatible with your own convictions and values.

Encouragingly, many are taking on that challenge.

While I was speaking in Portland, Oregon, a group of teenagers approached me after a *Why Wait?* talk at the fairground. They enthusiastically explained that they were part of an organisation of teenagers that speaks in schools on the advantages of abstinence. They shared that the *Why Wait?* campaign and book had helped them prepare their presentations.

Then they gave me one of their handouts listing just some of the advantages *they* see in premarital abstinence. They defined chastity as 'a virtue including sexual control or using one's sexual powers according to one's state in life. A virtue is a good habit.'

Their list of advantages for abstinence included:
1. Freedom from pregnancy and disease.
2. Freedom from the bother and danger of the pill and other contraceptives.
3. Freedom from the pressure to get married before

you are ready.
4. Freedom from abortion.
5. Freedom from the trauma of giving your baby up for adoption.
6. Freedom from exploitation by others.
7. Freedom from guilt, doubt, disappointment, worry and rejection.
8. Freedom to experience fuller communication in dating relationships.
9. Freedom to be in control of your life.
10. Freedom to focus energy on establishing and realising life goals.
11. Freedom to develop a respect for life.
12. Freedom to develop unselfish sensitivity.
13. Freedom to have greater trust in marriage.
14. Freedom to enjoy being a teenager.

As you think about the importance of teaching abstinence in our schools and youth clubs, it is good to recall these comments made by teenagers themselves. As one teenage girl put it to me so succinctly: 'Thank you for telling me it's OK to wait.'

It is in this positive context that I offer the following convincing reasons in favour of sexual abstinence outside marriage.

5
The Medical Benefits of Abstinence

Abstinence protects from both the fear of and the consequences of sexually transmitted diseases (STDs)

During the late sixties everyone was raving about the pill. Women were finally liberated from the fear of pregnancy, and now sex could be natural and unencumbered. What they didn't know about the sexual revolution is that pill-inspired casual sex would usher in one of the greatest epidemics of sexually transmitted diseases in history.

Today everyone is extolling the condom as the solution to the STD problem, and many people view it as a free ticket to promiscuity. But condoms are not the answer any more than the pill was. Sexually transmitted diseases are raging through the population like a firestorm. The only 100% effective way to avoid the fear and consequences of STDs is abstinence.

The condom is not a safe sex choice; it is dangerous and potentially fatal. Dr Harold Jaffee, chief of epidemiology for the Centers for Disease Control, states: 'You just can't tell people it's all right to do whatever you want so long as you wear a condom. (AIDS) is just too dangerous a disease to say that.'

Dr Theresa Crenshaw, past president of the American

Association of Sex Educators, Counsellors and Therapists, and member of the Presidential AIDS commission, says that, 'If the wrong information (about condoms) is given, the effort will fail. It will cause death rather than prevent it. . . . To say that use of condoms is 'safe sex' is in fact playing Russian roulette. A lot of people will die in this dangerous game.'

Telling a person who engages in high-risk behaviour to use a condom is like telling someone who is driving while drunk to use a seat belt.

'Abstinence-based sex education', writes paediatrician Dr S. DuBose Ravenel, 'is free of harmful side effects, while the birth control approach, if the proven association with increased rates of sexual activity is causal, is replete with dangerous effects. These include an increase in sexually transmitted diseases, including AIDS, increased pregnancies, various complications of early use of oral contraceptives, and increased risk of cervical cancer with early onset of sexual activity.'[7]

Dr Joe S. McIlhaney, a gynaecologist, explains, 'If sex is avoided until marriage and then engaged in only in marriage, all those sexually transmitted diseases would be of no importance at all because they could not enter into a closed circle relationship between husband and wife. Such an approach is (neither naive nor 'moralising', but it is) now necessary.'[8]

Even Planned Parenthood Federation of America's (PPFA) own Lou Harris Poll showed:

In evaluating arguments for delaying sex, teenagers say that the danger of catching sexually transmitted diseases and the danger of a pregnancy ruining one's life are two messages that are most likely to influence their peers. Sixty-five percent think that telling teenagers to worry about catching diseases like AIDS and herpes would be likely to influence them to wait to have sexual intercourse. Sixty-two percent think that telling them how a pregnancy could ruin their life would be effective.[9]

Abstinence is a health issue. There are fifty-two sexually transmitted diseases, and that gives you fifty-two good, positive, medical reasons to abstain.

Abstinence frees from the fear and consequences of pregnancy

Abstinence is the only method of birth control that is 100 percent effective and 100 percent free of side effects. The US Family Planning Perspectives, October 1986, reported on the percentage of single women under eighteen who had an unwanted pregnancy within the first twelve months of using contraceptives:

diaphragm, 31.6%
condom, 18.4%
pill, 11%
IUD, 10.5%
Spermicides, 34%
Rhythm, 33.9%

There is an emotional trauma in pregnancy for a teenager. It is best described by a girl who wrote: 'I used to think, ten years from now I'll be a woman of twenty-four. Now I think, I'll be twenty-four—and my child will be ten.' To have a child at such an early age limits for many years to come what a young mother is able to do—and the father too, if they choose to get married. Many of their early dreams will go unfulfilled.

The National Academy of Science, in the report, 'Legalised Abortion and the Public Health,' points out:

'There probably is no psychologically painless way to cope with an unwanted pregnancy whether it is voluntarily interrupted or carried to term'[10]

Abstinence frees from the dangers of various birth control methods

Some IUDs can be harmful, and the pill should be closely monitored, especially when used by teenagers—but these precautions are seldom considered. Even PPFA president Faye Wattleton admits, 'All contraceptive methods currently in use have serious drawbacks in their efficacy, safety and acceptability. The most effective methods, the pill and IUD, (both) have side effects.'[11]

Abstinence frees from the trauma of abortion

The responsibilities of pregnancy are often overlooked in the heat of passion. For a teenager, raising a child is a heavy financial and social burden. Giving the child up for adoption can leave a painful emotional scar. But perhaps the most terrible anguish associated with unwanted pregnancy is the trauma of abortion.

Abortion can solve the unwanted pregnancy situation for the moment, but it never resolves the guilt or breaks the bond between a mother and her baby. Dr Anna Speckhard studied the emotional impact of abortion on the mother. Although the women she studied came from diverse backgrounds, the reactions were almost identical:

81% reported preoccupation with the aborted child;
73% reported flashbacks of the abortion experience;
69% reported feeling of 'craziness' after the abortion;
54% recalled nightmares related to the abortion;

35% had perceived visitations from the aborted child;
23% reported hallucinations related to the abortion.

In Dr Speckhard's findings, 72 percent of the subjects
said they held no religious beliefs at the time of their abortions, and 96 percent, in retrospect, regarded abortion as
the taking of life or as murder.[12]

The report, 'Legalised Abortions and the Public Health'.
by the National Academy of Science, points out:

> Certain trends emerge from a review of the scientific literature
> on the mental health effects of abortion. Emotional stress and
> pain are involved in the decision to obtain an abortion, and
> these are strong emotions that surround the entire proce-
> dure. . . Medical complications associated with legal abortion
> may occur at the time of abortion (immediate), within thirty
> days following the procedure (delayed), or at some later time
> (late).[13]

Abortion is a painful procedure. Complications may
develop and the emotional fallout can be overwhelming.
M. Uchtman, Ohio director of Suiciders Anonymous, told
the Cincinnati City Council on September 1, 1981: 'Suiciders Anonymous, in a thirty-five-month period, reported
counselling 5,620 members in the Cincinnati, Ohio, area.
The members had attempted or were considering suicide.
Of these, 1,800 had had abortions, of whom 1,400 were
between 15 and 24 years old.'

The Alan Guttmacher Institute, the research arm of
PPFA, admitted: 'The health, social and economic consequences of teenage pregnancy are almost all adverse. Pregnancies that end in abortion or miscarriage are, at least,
upsetting and sometimes traumatic to the pregnant
woman.'[14]

Hall and Zissok, in their study, 'Psychological Distress

Following Therapeutic Abortion,' found that 'the trauma of abortion may have significant emtional sequelae (consequences).'[15] Kumar and Robson report in *Psychological Medicine* that 'eight of twenty-one women who had obtained a past abortion were found to be clinically depressed and anxious. In contrast, only eight of ninety-eight who had not had abortions were depressed.'[16]

Dr Bulfin, in the article 'A New Problem in Adolescent Gynecology' in the *Southern Medical Journal*, explains that some teenagers have significant post-abortion complications:

> As more abortions are being done in teenage girls than ever before, an unusually large number of complications are being seen by some private practitioners. Because many of these adolescent patients in whom complications develop do not return to the physicians who di the abortions, accurate data on the incidence of abortion complications are difficult to obtain. . . . The diversity of complications that can occur in teenage girls after legal abortion is startling.[17]

Dr Bulfin reports the wide range of traumas among women who suffer with complication from abortions:

	%
Damage to reproductive organs	42.6
Uterine rupture or perforation	5.6
Endometritis	13.0
Salpingitis, pyosalpinx	13.0
Cervical lacerations	11.0
Severe emotional and psychiatric problems	16.1
Haemorrhage, intractable	13.0
Pelvic pain and dyspareunia	11.1
Infertility and repeated miscarriage	7.4
Incomplete operations; subsequent passage of foetal parts and tissue	74.0
Bowel resection with colostomy	1.9

Dr Bulfin also related some sad case studies of abortion trauma:

- A seventeen-year old girl, nine weeks pregnant, had a suction abortion at a local clinic. Fever, chills and pelvic pain became progressively worse. . . . She was hospitalised when a pelvic mass failed to respond to antibiotic therapy, and laparotomy on the eighth day after abortion revealed a perforated uterus with massive pyosalpinx and pelvic abscesses, necessitating total hysterectomy. . . .
- A seventeen-year-old girl. . . suffered cervical lacerations and severe haemorrhage after a clinic abortion. . . . She suffered prolonged disability, remorse and guilt and regretted very much having had the procedure. In the four years since the operation she has been unable to become pregnant. . . .
- A sixteen-year old girl was seen the day after a suction curettage abortion. . . . She had been bleeding. . . . She evidently had had acute gonorrhoea when the abortion was done, and. . .pelvic pain, tenderness and dyspareunia persisted for many months afterwards.

None of them felt they had been afforded any meaningful information about the potential dangers of the abortion operation. Incongruously, some had actually stopped the birth control pill because they had read it was 'too dangerous', believing that since abortion was legal, it must be safe. . . .

Serious complications and even deaths may go unreported for the following reasons:

(1) There is no mandatory reporting of legal abortions and their results in most states;
(2) often the physician who does the abortion never knows of later complications;

(3) vital facts may be omitted from death certificates;
(4) the average physician will not report the complication because of the paperwork involved.

The teenager, frightened and mentally and physically traumatised by her abortion, will often not seek help until she is almost moribund. Her parents may be the last to know. . . .[18]

One of the great benefits of abstinence is that all of the tragic physical and emotional traumas of abortion are completely avoided.

6
The Emotional Benefits of Abstinence

Abstinence protects from sexual addiction

Psychologists and counsellors tell us that sexual addictions (sexual obsessiveness) are a fast-growing problem in society, and counselling sex addicts is an increasing trend. Whether sexual addiction is strictly psychological or a combination of psychological and physical problems, no one can say for sure at the moment; but it is a real addiction. Like compulsive eating, bulimia or anorexia, sexual addiction may be caused by mental trauma or personality disorders in a person's life.

Pornography is proving to be just as addictive for many people as drugs, alcohol or food. Premarital sex also can become addictive. Constant sexual stimulation causes chemical changes in the body just as other addictions. There is a need to have a physical relationship with someone in order to survive. Communication begins to disappear. Petting becomes a pattern, and it's hard to go back to just holding hands. Other areas of a relationship become obscured by the physical. One girl who was heavily into drugs wrote, 'Sex is like drugs. You keep wanting bigger highs. In fact, I think it made me do more drugs. I'd get high, and then I'd do some weird, kinky stuff. Regular sex wasn't enough. I'd do things I felt horrible about. Then I would do more drugs to take away the pain. It was a vicious circle.'

The only reward from sex outside a loving, trusting relationship is the physical high. When the sexual high becomes the goal, one can become addicted to the high. The high serves as a form of denial of reality, denial of the pain, and denial of the need for love and understanding and the intimacy that is sought in the relationship. The pain of coping with the drugs and the sex is easier than the pain of coping with a lonely life.

'Sexual addiction,' reports *USA Today*, 'is more apt to elicit snickers than concern. But addicts say it's no joke. And mental health professionals, increasingly concerned about the estimated thirteen million sex addicts in the United States, are determined to bring the compulsion out of the closet. Sexual addiction can lead to destruction.'[19]

The first forum on sex addiction took place in Los Angeles in 1989. The National Association on Sexual Addiction Problems reports:

'We live in a quick-fix society prone to using things like drinking, eating and sex as solutions to anxiety,' says Patrick Carnes, architect of the USA's first in-patient programme for sex addicts—the Sexual Dependency Unit at the Golden Valley (Minnesota) Institute for Behavioural Medicine. 'We are a very addictive culture.'

Although sex addicts can be news-making criminals, most aren't fringe characters.

'People have a picture of a sex addict in their minds,' says Golden Valley's Robin Anderson. 'The truth is most of the people are professionals with a devastating illness.'

A recent survey of fifty-four Golden Valley patients showed 42 percent earned more than £20,000 a year; 58 percent were college graduates. Equally revealing: As children, 74 percent had been sexually abused; 91 percent emotionally abused.

'The more you were abused as a child, the more addictions you will tend to have as an adult,' says Carnes.

Sexual addiction—whose symptoms can range from excessive masturbation to incest—can be as destructive as alcohol or drug addictions, often ruining careers and marriages.

Sex addicts often:

> Live a secret sexual life steeped in lies and shame;
> Find controlling urges nearly impossible;
> Pursue sexual interests obsessively despite personal and financial risks.

The obsessions have a way of staying underground.

'Our society likes to deny its sexuality and doesn't like hearing about sex offenders,' says Richard Salmon, executive director of the NASAP, Boulder, Colorado.[20]

Abstinence frees from the pressure to get married before one is ready

Premarital sex adds a sense of urgency to a relationship which is often vaguely expressed by one or both partners as a desire for greater commitment. Be it spoken or unspoken, the pressure for marriage is still there.

Physical intimacy cries out for emotional closeness and commitment. Yet those qualities are seldom present in a physically charged relationship. Indeed, they cannot be forthcoming without a lifetime commitment.

Abstinence frees from being put on a performance basis

Teenagers today are often put on a sexual performance basis; they must perform sexually if they are to be accepted. A performance-based relationship is one in which you are accepted for what you do, not for who you are.

When the physical performance becomes the standard for acceptance or rejection, fear is built into the relationship. Without the committed bonds of marriage, sex is inherently a selfish act done for personal gain. For a relationship based on performance to continue, the sex partners must continue to be pleasing to each other. As soon as one partner no longer lives up to what the other wants, the relationship is in trouble. Or if someone else comes along who has more of what the other is looking for in bed, the relationship takes a dive. The relationship is really one of mutual exploitation.

If her cute face and large breasts are what attracted him to her, when someone comes along with a cuter face or larger breasts she will be rejected. Performance partners keep each other in a state of perpetual insecurity, a state that symbolises much of what true love is not. Couples in these circumstances experience an unspoken element of fear: the fear of rejection.

Abstinence protects from comparison later in marriage

The famous psychologist Abraham Maslow once described sex as the peak of human emotions. The powerful emotions and memories of an illicit sexual encounter are forces a person may have to deal with for years after the actual event. I have counselled people who can describe the details of a number of sexual encounters, but they don't even remember their sex partners' names. Such is the influence sex has on our emotions and memories.

If a man becomes involved with someone in an intimate physical relationship so that he knows her physical qualities and points of sexual arousal, he will later compare his future wife to her. One woman wrote to me, 'My two friends must also deal with the problem of comparing their husbands to the men of their past relationships. Although guilt makes them feel hesitant or inhibited, they also fight the attitude of scorn or rejection for their husbands, who always seem to fall short, not measuring up to idealised memories of previous sexual encounters.'

A female student at the University of Chicago said to me, 'I've decided that I don't want to marry a virgin. I want to marry an experienced man, someone who knows what he's doing in bed.'

'You've got to be nuts, lady,' I replied. 'You're telling me that you want an experienced man who will know how to arouse you because that's how he aroused some other woman. He'll be comparing your breasts to her breasts, your thighs to her thighs, your ecstatic experience to her ecstatic experience. He'll be trying positions on you some other woman enjoyed.'

She immediately responded, 'I don't want that!'

Any girl who marries an experienced man will miss the joy of discovery and the bonding that takes place when a couple learn love-making together. She will always be just one of many.

The 'first-time' is something to be remembered. It is to be a wonderful time, something to look back upon as a symbol of fidelity. Sadly, for those who choose not to remain virgins, that first time with someone else will also always live in the memory.

Abstinence protects the most delicate sex organ: the mind

The most important sex organ is the mind. How does the mind relate to the loins? In this way: In the New Testament is one of the most profound verses ever written about marriage and sex: 'Let marriage be held in honour among all. Let the marriage bed be undefiled' (Hebrews 13:4). 'In honour' means in high esteem. The words 'marriage bed' in the Greek language literally mean 'sexual coitus'. The verse is saying, 'Let sexual coitus (intercourse) be pure, undefiled and unadulterated in the context of the marriage bed.'

What does it mean to be sexually pure? The word pure means 'no foreign element'. For example, an unopened bottle of aspirin is 100 percent aspirin—it's pure aspirin. But if someone comes along and injects arsenic into the bottle, the aspirin becomes impure, defiled or adulterated. Why? A foreign element entered the pure substance. The above passage says, 'Don't let any foreign element enter sexual coitus in your marriage bed.'

Men will say, 'What does my mind have to do with sex?'

A lot. The mind is the most powerful and most sensitive sex organ. Sex begins in the mind. Disconnect the mind and try to get aroused.

How does it work—sex and the mind? Why is it that we remember certain things and don't remember other things? Let's say somebody really embarrassed you a year ago. You can probably recall the face, the place and the event. But you probably can't remember who you had lunch with that day.

There are a number of explanations for our experiences with 'selective remembering'. One is that it's a biochemical reaction. Research shows that when we have an intense emotional experience involving the five senses, a chemical is released which implants that experience in our mind for recall. This biochemical reaction allows us to remember the significant events over the insignificant, the important over the unimportant.

Nothing triggers us biochemically quite like sex—starting with pornography. There are many men who are hooked on pornography. They can't go through a day without looking at it. Many can't even look at a woman without recalling pornographic images. Some distraught women have confessed that their husbands can't make love to them or have an orgasm without a picture of a nude woman on the pillow. Why? Because of the way these men have programmed their main sex organ—their mind.

Not only does pornography lodge in the memory, but past sexual experiences can too. A thirty-two-year-old man I've known for a number of years came to me in tears one day.

'What's wrong?' I asked.

'Josh, I need your help. You know that I've been married for eight years. I love my wife. There's nobody in the world as beautiful and sensitive as she. But in eight years of marriage, we've never been alone in bed.'

I knew what was coming, but I asked, 'What do you mean?'

He went on to say that in high school he had played around a lot sexually with a number of women. His behaviour carried over into the university where it got out of control. During his junior year he met his wife-to-be. They fell in love and got married a year after college.

At this point he was crying hard. 'Starting on our wedding night,' he continued, 'I began to experience reruns in the theatre of my mind. I can't even have sex with my own wife without thinking of those other women. I picture other women when I look at my wife. It's destroying the intimacy in our marriage.'

'Reruns in the theatre of my mind'—that says it all. Our mind is like a piece of film—it records everything. He couldn't control the flashbacks and it was tearing his life and his marriage apart.

One twenty-six-year-old woman who had been married three years wrote me: 'Josh, how do I get rid of the ghosts of relationships past?'

You see, you can date someone, become sexually involved and then break up. You can send back the fancy ring, you can cut his or her picture into a thousand pieces, and you can burn all the mementos, but you can't send back memories. Men and women don't forget sexual experiences—even when they want to.

Abstinence protects from misleading feelings

One solid reason for waiting is that sexual involvement, especially for teenagers, can produce confusion between sex and love. Premarital sex can terribly confuse a person who actually may have had a legitimate understanding of love. One writer said that sexual encounters outside marriage give an illusion of intimacy which can be mistaken for the lasting commitment that ultimately makes marriage work.

Often when sex enters into a relationship, the physical becomes its all-consuming element. The intellectual, emotional, social and spiritual all take a back seat to sex (no pun intended!). All the couple wants to do is spend time alone engaging in physical activity, and they mistake sex for love. Sadly and ironically, when one partner breaks off the relationship, he or she often can't stand to be near or talk to the other because the guilt feelings over the sexual activity are too strong. The guilt quickly washes away the false feelings of love.

Sex before marriage turns relationships upside down and mixes emotions to the point where a person can misinterpret feelings. A couple often becomes sexually involved and then misinterprets the act of sex and their own feelings. They think they 'know' the other person better than they really do. They think the relationship is deeper than it really is. They mistake their feelings for love and say 'I do.' But the marriage is probably doomed.

Don Smedley writes:

> When we mix sex and love, we confuse the simple concepts of giving and taking. Love always gives and always seeks the best interests of the other person. Premarital sex usually takes. Each individual has his or her own goal in having sex before marriage, but each is in it for personal reasons. The problem is that taking can sometimes look like the giving.

A girl may give her boyfriend 'what he wants,' thus making it look as though she is giving to him in love. But she does it from a personal motive. She may want the security he provides. She may want to achieve popularity by being his girlfriend. She may have one of a dozen other reasons, but her 'giving' is actually a form of taking. She is manipulating him for her own ends. She is being misled by her emotions.

Sex always changes the dynamics of a relationship.

Abstinence protects from sustaining 'bad' relationships

Breaking up from dating relationships or meaningful relationships can tear teenagers apart emotionally. We have all experienced the sadness of breaking off a relationship with someone we cared about but could no longer get along with. But when we add physical involvement, breaking emotional ties is even harder. Abstinence reduces the pain of breaking up.

So many people have said to me, 'When I walked away from that relationship, I left a part of me behind.' Sex forms a bond that can exist no matter what the rest of the relationship is like. Even if communication has broken down and emotions are strained, sex forms an almost unexplainable bond. It locks people into relationships. The longer it goes on, the harder it is to break it off and then leave it behind.

Abstinence frees from the trauma of having to give up a baby for adoption

One of the hardest decisions an unwed couple must make is giving up their out-of-wedlock child for adoption. Often, however, this is their only option. The financial responsibilities of parenthood make it almost impossible for teenagers to raise children, but the emotional tug, especially between mother and child, is very strong.

Abstinence helps avoid deep scars

'Love you for ever' feelings, which convince couples to think that premarital sex is OK, don't in fact last for ever. When couples engage in sex, they give a special part of themselves to each other. When they break up, that part which was given is lost—never to be regained. This type of emotional scarring can be very difficult to overcome.

Abstinence provides a basis of trust

Any marriage counsellor will tell us that trust is one of the most vital factors, if not the most vital one, in a fulfilled love, sex and marriage relationship. Abstinence protects from suspicion and distrust, and provides the trust needed for fulfilling love and sex in a marriage relationship.

In a study of students at Virginia Tech, one of the questions asked was, 'What is the number one thing you want in a relationship?' Do you know what came out? Trust. Far above anything else. At San Jose State University, fifty men and women did an article called, 'Sexual Liberation: Is It Worth the Hassle?' for a major women's magazine. These students concluded that sex wasn't worth the hassle without two basic ingredients: love and trust.

Where do suspicion and mistrust come from? They are often built into the relationship before marriage. If a person was sexually active before marriage, there is nothing to guarantee he or she won't be promiscuous after marriage. Commitment might change at the altar, but personality doesn't change. As the years go by, many who had roving eyes before marriage find their eyes roving again. The seeds of suspicion and mistrust, which were hidden and unspoken all along, begin to sprout. Once trust is gone, so is the marriage.

After two, three or four years of marriage, the mind starts playing tricks: *If she slept with someone before, will she now? If he played around before, can I trust him now?* And when there's distrust in the relationship, it is impossible to be vulnerable. How can one open oneself up to somebody without 100 percent trust? Intimacy goes right out the window. Fulfilling love and sex in marriage start with trust.

I never dreamed that the way I treated a woman on dates some twenty years ago would affect my marriage today, but it does. As a graduate student I dated a young lady named Paula for more than three years. We almost got married, and then we realised we weren't in love. We didn't have the kind of love needed to build a lasting, deep, intimate, marriage-sex-family relationship. We just liked each other and had a good time together. But you don't get married on that.

So we broke off our relationship. It was one of the hardest things I've ever done in my life. I felt when I walked away from Paula, I was walking away from everything I'd ever dreamed of in a woman. I thank God now; but it was hard then. It tore me apart. Paula and I did remain friends, and to this day she is one of my dearest, closest friends.

Several years later I met Dottie, and she became my wife. Dottie then met Paula. They became friends, really hit it off, and started to spend time together. One morning Dottie came home from having breakfast with Paula and said, 'Honey, I'm so glad you behaved yourself for those three-and-a-half years.'

'What do you mean?'

'Paula shared with me this morning that there were times when she was so in love with you she would have done anything, and you never once took advantage of her.'

I breathed a sigh of relief and was extremely thankful.

You cannot imagine what it meant to my wife to know: *I can trust my husband*. I never realised that the way I treated a woman on a date would contribute one of the most positive factors in my marriage to Dottie. My wife trusts me, and trust is one of the greatest motivations for fidelity and faithfulness in marriage.

Abstinence helps develop respect for life

The realisation that one will never need to have an abortion, the commitment to abstinence, will help produce a new respect for the dignity of human life. When an unmarried girl is pregnant and considering abortion, she is under the binding pressure of thinking about the life of her child. By saying no to premarital sex, she won't ever have to rationalise her thoughts in order to justify an abortion.

Abstinence frees one to focus energy on establishing and realising life goals

When a teenager becomes a mother or father, their life dreams and ambitions, to all intents and purposes, must be put on hold indefinitely if not for ever. Of course for some, motherhood and fatherhood is a way of escape from a lonely existence. The sad fact is that the attention they may receive after the baby comes is short-lived and the reality of raising the child sets in. It can be all the more troubling if friends move away or go on to other things.

A teenager told me recently that her friend had a baby, and that she never has time for herself. She can't go places she would normally go and her evenings are always spoken for. Those who follow abstinence and stay away from premarital sex can focus their drives and energy on dreams and aspirations. Every student, every athlete and every businessman or woman who ever made it had dreams and goals.

Abstinence gives freedom from guilt

Guilt is a consequence of premarital sex that can haunt a person for a very long time, and perhaps offers the best reason for waiting until marriage. The emotional and psychological distress is very real, and a crippling guilt with little joy can be the result.

Whatever people may say about guilt, it is real. As psychologist Erich Fromm said, 'It is indeed amazing that, in as fundamentally irreligious a culture as ours, the sense of guilt should be so widespread and deep-rooted.'[21]

Why does guilt follow promiscuity? True guilt comes from the awareness of having transgressed a standard of right and wrong. If waiting for sex until marriage is God's standard, we will experience guilt when we violate it, even if only for a short time, because we refuse to face the issue and admit the guilt.

False guilt comes from outside influences, such as other people who try to make us feel guilty when there is no reason for us to feel that way. For example, friends may make us feel guilty for missing their party when we chose to do something else that we needed to do. Going to the party would have violated what we felt was right. If we had given in to friends and not listened to our own conscience, our guilt would have been valid.

Unless guilt is dealt with, it can be a heavy burden. Only through a personal relationship with Christ can true guilt be dealt with and false guilt be avoided.

Feelings of guilt and hurting consciences are two of the most common results of premarital sex teenagers talk about in their letters. One girl told me that the guilt from a few minutes of sexual pleasure destroyed a year's worth of fun, happy times and good memories.

Manhatten sex therapist Shirley Zussman comments about the inner hurt which results from premarital sex: 'Being part of a meat market is appalling in terms of self-esteem.' Dr Elizabeth Whelan, in her book *Sex and Sensibility*, cites a study of unmarried women which showed that 85 percent of those under psychiatric care were sexually active.[22]

A faculty member at the Univerity of Wisconsin (Madison) explained to me that a study showed 86 percent of psychologists' patients who were interviewed had engaged in premarital sex. Their main problem was guilt caused by those acts.

A man in Tucson speaks frequently to health and family classes at the University of Arizona. In 1970, 1975 and 1980 he surveyed hundreds of students in his seminars. He asked them, 'If you have had sexual intercourse outside marriage, what were the results?' The answers showed:

	Male	Female	Total
Tremendous guilt	50%	63%	57%
Led to break up	50	26	38
Created intense desire for more	44	26	35
Increased sexual frustration and pressure	33	26	30
Felt used	17	42	30

It seems obvious that premarital sex and emotional instability are related.

Abstinence helps develop unselfish sensitivity

When a person is not operating under guilt, he is free to give to others. Avoiding premarital sex enables teens to focus more on others and their needs. They are not forced into trying to meet needs that cannot possibly fulfil this side of marriage.

7

Relational Benefits of Abstinence

Abstinence enhances true communication in a relationship

Not only does premarital sex cloud the issue of true love, but it also tends to thwart the communication process. Most of us by nature gravitate towards what comes easily and is pleasurable. Therefore, sex offers an easy out to those who have never learned to communicate intimately apart from the physical. Many people believe that sex produes intimacy, but William McCready of the School of Social work at the University of Chicago points out, 'Sexual activity only celebrates what's there. Sex cannot deliver what doesn't already exist.'

Hunger for an intimate relationship is built into each of us. We all want to love and be loved. Sex is merely the physical expression of that intimate love we seek, not the source of it. That is why premature sex will shortcut an immature relationship. It tries to express something that isn't there yet.

In a survey of more than 700 US sex therapists and counsellors, 85 percent said that the number one complaint they hear is lack of communication in relationships. Of the 30,000 women who took this survey, most said they had chosen their husbands based on sex appeal, but 80 percent said if they had to do it over again, they would choose a husband based on his ability to communicate.

Immature lovers (which everyone is at the beginning) get confused about the differences between the sex act and real communication. They think they are the same. (This is a pattern often begun early in their relationship when they confuse sex with love.) But true sharing between two people is much, much more than just sex. Outside marriage, the genuine communication upon which a mature relationship should grow is lost while the couple concentrates on a shallow substitute.

Abstinence helps build patience and self-control

Patience and self-control are major building blocks in a maximum love, marriage and sexual relationship. The media says 'hurry up' to everything, especially sex. I say 'wait' and in so doing you build the discipline of patience and concern. Those guided by lust and the inability to wait, will be crippled in their marriage. In marriage there are many times when patience is needed, especially in the sexual area. A partner may be ill, and the other must wait for sex until he or she feels better. A job may require one partner to travel, and patience and self-control can build in a tremendous trust factor with one's spouse. Failure to develop patience and self-control before marriage, impatience and lack of control will carry over into every aspect of life, especially marriage.

Abstinence helps to enhance a special relationship found only in a marriage

The unique oneness, the joy of fidelity and the bond of love and trust found in a marriage where each waited for sex until he or she was married is a case where 'the whole is much greater than the sum of the parts'. It is indeed a special relationship. Waiting to be physically intimate until marriage doesn't guarantee a great marriage—but the joys, the pleasures and the trust which are built will surpass anything one could possibly imagine.

Sexual promiscuity does not exclude anyone from a fulfilled love, marriage and sexual relationship. However, premarital sex can add many negative factors that will be difficult to overcome. No one will miss out on anything if they wait, but if they don't wait, they can miss out on something wonderful.

Abstinence helps develop positive principles of relational growth

Abstinence encourages growth in the areas of discovering who each person is and what each personality is like and in developing real friendship. This is far more important than sex to a successful, life-long relationship. In fact, it is the real basis for great sex in marriage. Abstinence creates and encourages more time for talking, building mutual interests and spending time with other friends. Through abstinence it is possible to develop an intimacy that is more than physical.

Abstinence provides freedom to enjoy being a teenager

This is one of the most important reasons for abstinence. Staying uninvolved sexually allows a youngster to enjoy a healthy and fun-loving time as a teenager. The pressure of premarital sex is not healthy. It can add undue pressure and frustration.

Abstinence provides one of the greatest gifts of true love: virginity

One of the greatest gifts one can give a future mate is one's own sexual fidelity. I have never heard anyone complain because he (or she) waited to have sex with the person he married. No one! Yet I know countless heartbroken teenagers who wished they had waited. What a contrast!

Many of those who didn't wait felt they needed the practice, needed to master the technique. Nothing could be further from the truth—the plumbing almost always works. More important, the sexual patterns one builds with someone other than one's mate can infect marriage later on. Learning about sex together provides a bonding that ultimately can be enjoyed and appreciated only in a faithful marriage.

Some may already have lost their physical virginity and it can never be recovered. But they can start over again right where they are and practice 'secondary virginity.' Most of the 'plus factors' of abstinence can be true in life again. Those who haven't lost their virginity need to remember that it's something that cannot be recovered. There is only one 'first time'.

A while back I received the following letter:

I'm a seventeen-year-old virgin. I'm a high school senior. My friends make jokes about my virginity. They often make remarks about my 'lack of experience'. The pressure gets pretty great.

So last Tuesday, when I had lunch at school with five of my girlfriends, I said, 'Look, I don't want any more pressure about me becoming sexually involved. I don't want any more jokes about my virginity. Each of you needs to realise that, whenever I want to, I can become like you, but you can never again become like me.'

That's a powerful way for a teenager to cope with sexual peer pressure, and I thank God for youngsters who are taking a stand like this in schools and colleges today.

8
Personal Benefits of Abstinence

Abstinence helps increase self-esteem

People are not really seeking sex today—they're seeking intimacy. They look to sex as a means to gain that closeness, but it doesn't work. It can't work outside a committed marriage relationship. Why? Because sex as it should be in marriage is based on security. There is a need for total love, companionship and freedom in giving to each other sexually. The marriage is designed to be a permanent commitment in which the partners are completely secure. There is no need to prove anything, no need for ego-boosts, no cause for insecurity. The relationship provides mutual trust and unconditional love and thus an atmosphere of understanding, acceptance and intimacy.

When this intimacy is attempted in a relationship without the marriage commitment, it is usually doomed to fail. No lasting trust can be forged without commitment. Yet many people try, and in doing so only further damage their sense of self-worth. If they get into a relationship looking for intimacy and then fail to achieve it, which is often the case, their already low self-esteem spirals even lower. They feel incapable of being loved and incapable of truly loving anyone. They seek emotional intimacy through physical intimacy—and they never achieve it.

The modus operandi becomes, 'It's easier to bare your bottom than bare your soul.' Then, in the words of family, child and marriage counsellor Dick Day, 'Your body becomes a psychological barrier.'

Abstinence can be a good 'test' of love

In response to the cheap, self-centred pressure line, 'If you really love me, you will,' one can say, 'If you really love me you'll wait.' Abstinence tests the feelings beyond the first attraction, whether physical or emotional.

Abstinence can make better lovers

It encourages us to explore a greater variety of ways to express love and our sexual desires.

Abstinence can be an expression of emotional integrity

A high school health education teacher asked his three health classes to come up with reasons teenagers should say no to sex. The following list of reasons was mailed to me by the instructor.

1. To avoid teenage pregnancy.
2. To avoid STDs.
3. I don't want to feel guilty.
4. I don't want a reputation where dates expect sex and date me only for that reason.
5. I would disappoint my parents and would lose their trust and respect.
6. I might lose respect for the other person, they might lose respect for me, and I might lose respect for myself.
7. Sex is better in a secure, loving relationship like marriage.

8. The thought of having an abortion scares me to death.

9. Sex gets in the way of real intimate communication.

10. Sexual relationships are a lot harder to break up even when you know you should.

11. It may ruin a good relationship rather than make it better.

12. There are better ways to get someone to like you.

13. You won't have to worry about birth control side effects.

14. I'm not emotionally ready for that intense a relationship.

15. I could become scared of my partner.

16. I don't want to hurt someone I really care about.

17. Sex could become the central focus of the relationship, like an addiction. At that point it's no longer a meaningful relationship, but you are using each other to satisfy desires.

18. You begin to compare sexual experiences leading to lots of disappointments.

19. I don't want to make myself vulnerable to being used or abused sexually.

20. If I'm hurt too many times, I might miss out on something great because I'm afraid of being hurt again.

21. I like my freedom too much. Sexual relationships are too binding.

22. I'm only sixteen.

23. I'm proud of my virginity and I want it to stay that way. (This was shared by a boy and a girl.)

24. Building a relationship in other ways is more important.

25. I don't want to risk becoming someone's sex object.

26. I want my first experience to be a good one with someone who won't laugh at me, reject me, tell lies about me, and who I know will be there tomorrow.

27. It's possible to enjoy ourselves physically without going all the way.

28. Why rush something that could be lousy or mediocre now, when it could be great later?

29. I don't want sex to lose its meaning and value so that I feel 'sexually bankrupt.'

30. I am afraid that at this age it might not meet up to my expectations and I may be seriously disappointed.

31. I don't want to risk ending a relationship and hating each other because of it.

32. I might find it painful and the other person rough and uncaring.

33. It may only serve for the boy to brag about scoring with you.

34. It's the safest way not to become pregnant.

35. You may feel invaded and you can't take it back after it's happened to you.

36. You may have to grow up too fast and too soon.

37. Sex may become the only thing that keeps the relationship together.

38. You may have sex too early to really enjoy or understand it.

39. You lose the chance to experience the 'first time' with someone who really cares for you.

40. I want my most intimate physical relationship to be with the one I marry.

41. Sex brings feelings of jealousy, envy, and possessiveness.

9
Examining The Curriculum

Circular 5/94, Education Act 1993: Sex Education in Schools published 6th May 1994 by the British government requires that all state schools revise their sex education programmes so that instruction takes place in a clear moral framework. Governors of primary schools must decide whether or not to have a sex education programme beyond what is required in the National Curriculum Science Orders. Secondary Schools must offer a programme of sex education to all pupils, including teaching on STDs. Parents have the right to withdraw their children at all phases of sex education if they so wish. However, schools are encouraged to consult with parents in order to produce an acceptable policy.

If we are to promote abstinence-based sex education then we must look carefully at the programmes currently being used in our schools. Any parent who is not worried about the problem of sexual promiscuity among young people is either naive or insensitive. The statistics (121,000 teenage pregnancies in the UK in 1988, one third of which were terminated) only begin to hint at the suffering, the sorrow, the ruined lives that are the inevitable by-product of an increasingly permissive society. For every unmarried teenage couple 'in trouble', there are usually two sets of parents, grandparents, and brothers and sisters who are potential co-sufferers, as well as family friends and school mates. There are also the children of such liaisons, surely the greatest sufferers of all and the most blameless.

But pregnancy is no longer the only worry among those concerned about teenage promiscuity. Sexually transmitted diseases increasingly pose a threat to the health and lives of all who engage in irresponsible sexual behaviour, and young people are increasingly at risk. The permissiveness of Western society over the past twenty years has exposed a generation of teenagers to a variety of medical dangers that were known in an earlier time only to the most jaded and irresponsible of adults. And there is no reason to believe that things are improving significantly. Indeed some medical authorities predict that promiscuous conduct among young people will become even more dangerous than it is today.

Changing values

It is understandable that in the wake of such social devastation educators are attempting to devise ways in which the schools can help the family in this area—and the result has been a renewed push for required sex education in the classroom.

One can sympathise however with those parents who are reluctant to see the educational system assume the burden of sex education at this particular moment in our history. They may have no objections to such courses offering sex education of a certain sort and indeed, such courses can perform a useful service to the community. For example, there may be no reason why young people of thirteen or fourteen should not receive basic instruction on human sexuality in their biology classes. Taught in the same way that other systems of the body are taught, these classes can teach young people all they need to know about the physiological aspects of the subject. Such information is useful and can be presented objectively and scientifically.

But to stress the idea that young people have a 'right' to be 'sexually active' if they want to; that society has no legitimate role in prescribing sexual conduct for its members; to offer explicit and detailed instruction in erotic behaviour—all this can be very damaging to young people and contribute to the permissive atmosphere that exists in our society today.

Excluding parents

We need also to be concerned about the failure of many schools to share their plans for sex education with parents. For example, in one widely used curriculum in the USA the following note appears in the opening section:

> How to Begin the Programme: Caution: participants should not be given extra copies of the form to show to their parents or friends. Many of the materials of the programme, shown to people outside the context of the programme itself, can evoke misunderstanding and difficulties.

This popular programme includes highly explicit colour slides of both heterosexual and homosexual intercourse, as well as audio cassettes of homosexual males and lesbians who talk about the pleasure and satisfaction they derive from their deviant behaviour. One of the stated purposes of this programme is, 'To make clear that sexual relationships with the same sex during youth are normal and do not necessarily indicate one's future sexual orientation as an adult.'

Small wonder the author warns that these materials, shown to parents, 'can evoke. . .difficulties'.

Other texts are similarly cautionery in their instructions

to teachers. Some even suggest that the very purpose of the programme would be subverted were parents to be informed about course contents, since, as a recent programme puts it: 'One of the primary developmental tasks for teenagers is to separate from their parents.' If 'to separate from their parents' means to adopt a different set of moral values, then I believe the state school system has no business deliberately encouraging students to do such a thing.

Fortunately, most schools in the USA and in the UK are respectful of what the community believes and go out of their way to make sex education curricula compatible with family values. If, however you should live in one of those communities where the schools have initiated programmes at variance with your religious or moral beliefs, then you may need to take one of several steps to make certain that your children are not subjected to potentially unhealthy indoctrination.

Examine the contents

The first step in determining the nature of your children's sex education programme is to examine the contents.

If you don't feel competent to judge the quality of bias of the materials, then ask for help from someone whose opinion you value. For example, you might enlist your pastor, since clergy usually have the training and critical judgement to assess the meaning of the written word. If you know other parents who share your concern, then ask one or more of them to join you in this evaluation.

When you have decided who is to accompany you, then call and make an appointment with the teacher or school nurse in charge of the programme. Be as polite and as specific as possible. Tell the instructor you are interested in what kind of sex education your child is receiving and would like to look over the materials used. Ask if your child can bring home a copy of the materials before your meeting so that you can review everything at your leisure. Be sure to ask for video cassettes and audio tapes as well, since they are often the most vivid and provocative materials used.

If the instructor agrees to furnish these materials and gives you everything you ask for, the chances are you have little to worry about. Most of the genuinely destructive programmes warn the teacher to keep texts and tapes from parents at all costs. However, when you receive the materials, examine them carefully, noting questionable or objectionable segments.

In so doing, don't be *too* picky. Chances are that even the instructor doesn't think the programme is perfect; and if you quibble over minor points, you may forfeit your credibility when you address major issues.

If the instructor refuses to send the materials home, then ask that they be assembled for you when you have your meeting. Be sure to reserve at least an hour so you will have time enough to review everything used in the course. Ask if there are copying facilities available in case you want to reproduce a page for closer scrutiny.

Ask questions

In evaluating materials in your discussions with the instructor you should ask the following questions:

1. Does the programme encourage young people to engage in sexual intercourse or does it send a clear message of abstinence and self-restraint?

Many bad programmes mention abstinence in an inital sentence or two, then devote the balance of their presentation to a discusssion of erotic behaviour in explicit detail. Balance and proportion are important elements to consider in evaluating the total impact of sex education materials.

2. Does the programme violate community standards of taste and decency?

This is a difficult question to answer objectively, and you should not make the mistake of assuming that what you find indelicate or insensitive would necessarily offend a substantial portion of the community. So you might want to seek help from a cross-section of your friends. Ask others what they think. Listen carefully to their answers. Write them down. In discussing this criterion with instructors or administrators it is much better to say, 'Ten people I questioned found this passage objectionable,' than to say, 'This passage offended me'.

3. Does the programme present traditional viewpoints of sexuality as well as those of more permissive individuals and organisations? If so, does it present them in comparable detail with the same degree of objectivity or sympathy?

Again, these are difficult questions to answer, and you should be careful to use criteria that are as logical and unbiased as possible: amount of space (or time) devoted to each point of view, the use of 'weighted' language, the presentation of all available evidence. For example, in examining programmes that touch on the subject of birth control devices, you should make certain that negative as well as positive statistics appear. According to generally accepted studies, the failure rate of condoms to prevent pregnancy is 10 percent overall and 18 percent for women in their middle and late teens. And there is reason to believe the failure rate in the prevention of diseases such as AIDS may be the higher of these two figures. These studies should be cited in discussing such an important issue as birth control and disease prevention.

4. What selection process was used in choosing this particular programme?

It is important to find out whether or not other programmes were considered. If they were, you might want to see if any were 'abstinence programmes'. Ask for specific names of curricula that were rejected. Then ask for the criteria used in making a final decision. If other options were not explored, you should ask why.

Also, you should ask who was involved in the selection process. Were outside 'experts' consulted, and if so, who were they and how were they chosen?

If you feel the process has been unfair, you might want to give the instructor or principal information concerning programmes that emphasise abstinence. These have increased in popularity over the past few years, largely because of their measurable success. (In America, for example, Teen-Aid, an abstinence programme used at San Marcos (California) Junior High School, reports a reduction of pregnancies from 147 in the 1984-85 school year to 20 in 1986-87. When asked, 'Are you now more willing to say "No" to sex before marriage?' 69 percent of students completing the Sex Respect programme answered affirmatively, as opposed to 16 percent at the beginning of the programme.)

5. What is the purpose of the programme now in place?

There are many possible answers to this question and in some cases several of them could apply. One answer might be: 'To teach teenagers the biological facts of reproduction.' Another might be: 'To teach young people to abstain from sexual intercourse until maturity and marriage.' Still another might be: 'To teach students to minimise the dangers of pregnancy and disease while engaging in premarital intercourse.' One of the common answers given to explain the more destructive programmes goes something like this; 'To teach young people to clarify their own values concerning sexuality so they can make intelligent decisions regarding their own conduct.' Such an approach—the so-called 'values-clarification' approach—is deceptive in its appeal to fairness and objectivity. In fact, values-clarification curricula usually tell young people that they can do anything they want to with little or no regard for parental or societal inhibitions.

One of the pioneers of this approach in the USA, educational psychologist W.R. Coulson, has termed such education a failure and has said of the student exposed to it: 'The outcome (confirmed in the research) is that he's become more likely to give in to what before he would have regarded as temptation to be resisted. Now he sees it as a developmental task, a "risk of further growth."' In dealing with such programmes you should ask instructors and administrators whether or not they would apply the same 'even-handed approach' to such issues as murder and racism.

Teenage sexuality is a major problem today largely because too many young people think they have the right to make decisions for themselves, even though they are in no position to bear the financial and emotional costs of pregnancy or a sexually transmitted disease such as AIDS. To suggest they are mature enough to decide about such questions independent of community codes and norms is to fly in the face of all the statistics (which have been collected in recent years) on pregnancy and disease.

Be sure that the stated purpose of the programme is comprehensive enough to explain those parts you find most objectionable. If the official purpose of the programme is 'to teach young people the basic biological facts about human reproduction' then it is justifiable to ask why entire segments are devoted to such subjects as homosexual conduct and petting.

Approaching the Head Teacher

If the instructor refuses to show you the programme or if you have questions that remain unanswered, then you probably need to talk to the Head Teacher of the school. Some Heads keep a close watch on the classroom activity of their teachers while others try to give instructors a freer rein. There are arguments in favour of both approaches. However, every good Head Teacher should be concerned when parents believe something is going on in the school that undermines the values of the community. If you have such a complaint, in all likelihood the Head would prefer that you voice it directly rather than repeat it throughout the community. So when you call for an appointment, you should specify exactly what is bothering you and give an account of your efforts to resolve your doubts about the programmes.

In setting up the appointment remember that your best approach will be in the role of a parent seeking information rather than as someone who already has all the answers and wants to pick a fight. If you come to the Head as a calm and reasonable person, then your own position on these matters will seem more credible.

At the same time, you should make your own position clear from the outset and give the distinct impression that you are interested in all the facts before you decide what to do about the problem. Perhaps the Head Teacher is likewise worried about this particular course or instructor. Per-

haps your concerns are precisely what is needed to gener-
ate some action. Don't assume that the Head will necessarily prove to be an adversary, but be prepared for anything. A good Head Teacher will back up an experienced
teacher until given sufficient reason to do otherwise.

If you have not been granted access to the materials used
in the class then request that the Head Teacher obtain the
texts and tapes for you. Explain that you are simply trying
to determine what is going on in that particular class or
unit, that the subject matter includes sensitive materials
about which any responsible parent should be concerned.

Legal aspects and actions

If the Head Teacher refuses to intervene in your behalf to
obtain the materials, then you have a right to know why. He
may reply that the instructor is merely exercising his or her
academic freedom in choosing materials without interference from parents. Such an argument may or may not be
legally defensible. While teachers usually have some lee-
way to choose course materials, in many cases the local
authority prescribes certain approaches and publishes a list
of approved texts, particularly in the field of sex education.
You might write or call your Local Education Authority or
even the Department of Education to find out what laws
and procedures are in force.

Avoid confrontation if at all possible. Most teachers and
Heads are reasonable when faced with a strong and
unswerving will: and I am willing to bet that if you continue to go through the proper channels, you will eventually get what you want without threats of legal action.
Heads are more likely to be pragmatic and accommodating
than teachers, though such is not always the case.

The School Advisor

If your Head Teacher is adamant and confrontational, then you may want to talk with your local authority School Advisor. The Advisor is responsible for what happens to the schools in a Local Education Authority.

Most School Advisors have come up through the system, been teachers and Heads, and therefore have a certain sympathy for those under their jurisdiction. On the other hand, Advisors are usually more experienced and therefore more likely to know the limits to which a classroom teacher is entitled to go in the use of questionable materials and in the encouragement of values contrary to those of parents.

If you have followed the chain of command, then you should be able to gain an appointment with your Advisor (or with a key staff member) and to make the source of your dissatisfaction clear. The Advisor can assess the validity of your case, then interview the Head Teacher and make whatever recommendations seem appropriate under the circumstances.

The School Governors

If you don't get anywhere with your Advisor, you should consider visiting a member of the Board of Governors. If you live in a small town, you may know one of these people personally; but if you don't know any member, or if you live in a larger city, you should make inquiries and find out who on the board is most traditional in opinion and in voting habits. Then call and make an appointment.

Remember that it is not ordinarily the function of a School Governor to intervene in the day-to-day operations of the school. However, Governors have specific responsibilities and powers to produce a sex education policy for the school, and one that is biased towards traditional moral values.

Meeting the arguments

It may be that you will meet with various arguments aimed at deterring you from further 'interference'. The following may help:

1. 'Parents don't know enough about education to speak with any authority. Only professional educators have enough experience to make decisions on curricular matters.'

The question of what kind of sex education to offer in schools is a matter of great concern to all citizens, since it involves the basic values of the community rather than such purely academic considerations as teaching methodology. It's one thing to argue that schools should teach biology or sex education, and quite another to maintain that young people should be taught that sexual intercourse prior to marriage is a matter of 'personal choice' and that homosexuality is a 'normal and even desirable lifestyle'.

In order to clarify this point, let's take an example in another area—that of racial prejudice. It is one thing for schools to decide that a course in race relations should be taught, quite another to argue for an approach that stresses the right of each student to his own opinion on the question of bigotry, or which suggests that Martin Luther King and Hitler represent two equally valid 'alternate lifestyles'.

The truth is, racism is bad for society. It causes terrible problems and eventually costs human lives. It goes against the basic tenets of religious heritage, as summarised in the Golden Rule. But even if there were no religious principles involved, racism would still be destructive to the community and therefore a bad attitude to condone.

Likewise, sexual licence is bad for society. It causes terrible problems and eventually costs human lives (thousands have died of AIDS). It too goes against the basic tenets of our religious faith. But even if there were no religious principles involved, sexual promiscuity would still be destructive to the community and therefore a bad attitude to condone.

Parents know just as much about what is and isn't good for society as teachers do; and while parents can't prescribe teaching methods or particular textbooks, they can certainly give expert testimony on what teenagers should believe and how the wrong kind of sex education can undermine family values.

You might also want to remind the board that they too are not trained experts, yet sit in judgement on everything that happens in a school system, including classroom activities. They, like parents, must judge the larger consequences of what's being taught in the schools; so they, least of all, have the right to question the qualifications of those parents who intelligently monitor what's going on.

2. *'All the experts agree that explicit and 'non-judgemental' sex education courses are the best and most effective means of preventing unwanted pregnancies and sexually transmitted diseases.'*

There is virtually no educational issue of any consequence on which 'all the experts agree'—and certainly not this one. A number of experts are highly critical of programmes that tell young people sexual promiscuity is a valid option for them and that all they need to do is take certain precautionary measures to avoid 'undesirable consequences'.

For example, after examining a number of alternatives, a team of researchers at the US Department of Education recommended abstinence programmes as the best means of combating AIDS among young people.

Dr Melvin Anchell, psychiatrist and author of several books on human sexuality, has written: 'Some educators have a compulsion to teach sex, beginning with the three-year-old and continuing until high school graduation. Paradoxically, the effects of their schooling produce the very abnormalities that parents, and, perhaps, some well-meaning sex educators, wish to prevent.'

Devoid of real clinical experience and, in some cases, sexual maturity, sex educators can cause severe maladjustments by undue meddling.

Psychoanalysis has established that the period in a child's life between the ages of six and twelve is asexual; that is, a period during which sensual pleasures are normally repressed. . . . The period is well-recognised by psychiatrists throughout the world and has been designated as the 'latency period'. . . . During latency, the first stirring of compassionate feelings arises from the human mind. . . . This valuable instinct is dangerously jeopardised by sexually stimulating children in latency. Such interferences can prevent the 'capability' to feel compassion. The results can be increasingly noted in the antisocial behaviour of sexually 'over-stuffed' youths.

In natural development, pre-teen children derive sexual pleasures from sensual excitements caused by sexual fantasies. Sex educators who catapult the child into a world of authoritative sexual knowledge shatter these normal fantasy satisfactions. . . . Later in life, drugs and pornography are used as adjuncts to help recapture the pleasures from thwarted childhood fantasies that had not been allowed to resolve naturally.

By their own example, normal parents teach children that sex is a one-woman/one-man affair. The sex educator's advice, 'Sex is for fun', desecrates the affectionate and monogamous nature of human sexuality.

William R. Coulson, noted psychologist, has said: 'Society ought to be paying more attention to parental perspective right now, not waiting for the backlash. Science supports mothers and fathers in wanting their children spared the trials of sexual precocity, AIDS or not. And it supports the children in asking not to be underestimated. Self-discipling isn't beyond them, if they're told the truth .... The truth is summed up in six words: 'Abstinence before marriage, fidelity within it'.... Our children and grandchildren don't deserve to be judged sexually insatiable.'

These are but three examples of a growing body of opinion that supports not only the possibility but the appropriateness of sex education based on traditional morality. These experts, whatever their religious backgrounds, are speaking as professional educators (or therapists) who base their conclusions on scientific data as well as years of experience in their respective fields. They are distinguished by any objective standards, yet they voice the same concerns about permissive sex education that traditional-minded parents have been expressing. And there are many other educators and psychologists who share these views.

Of course, those who defend such education usually try to discount such authorities by saying that they are 'not respectable', that 'nobody takes them seriously', that 'their methodology is flawed'. If you are met by such a response, you can reply either by demanding that they prove such a statement right there on the spot, or by pointing out that this is precisely what your authorities say about their authorities; no side has a monopoly on the experts. Therefore, the question must be decided on other than 'scientific' grounds. At this point you can begin to talk about the rights of parents to teach a morality at home that is not systematically contradicted at school.

3. 'Anyone who opposes "explicit, non-judgemental sex education" in school is a right-wing extremist.'

If you have to deal with such name-calling then you are in for a very difficult time. This kind of argument is neither fair-minded nor intelligent. Usually it reveals a loss of patience or else an inability to continue the debate on an intellectual level. Phrases like 'right-wing extremist', 'bigot', and 'moralist' indicate no more than animosity. They don't answer legitimate arguments or counter persuasive evidence, and you must make that point to the person who tries to avoid a discussion of the issues by calling you names. Ask politely but firmly that the discussion be confined to the issues and that everyone avoid personal attacks, not only because they are rude and uncivil but because they are illogical—examples of the fallacy called 'ignoring the question'.

4. 'You are the only parents who have raised any complaints about this programme.'

Of course, it's possible that you are; but what does that prove? It may simply mean that other parents don't know what is going on in the classroom. You might want to ask the board if they have any objections to your sending a copy of the materials to all the parents in your child's class and ask them for comments. If the board says 'no objections', then do it. If they say 'we object', then you have a right to question their suggestion that you constitute an insignificant minority of parents.

You might also ask them if they believe the majority is always right. If they say 'no', then thank them for conceding your point. If they say 'yes', then ask them if they will be willing to decide the fate of this programme by a vote of all concerned parents, with a majority deciding the issue.

However, it is much better to answer this objection by making certain that you are not the only person present at the board meeting. You should try to persuade as many people as possible to join you in voicing any objections. In the first place, there is nothing so intimidating to members of an elected (or appointed) board as a large delegation prepared to protest board actions or school policy. Numbers suggest not only widespread concern but also a certain intensity of commitment, since it takes a lot to move people to come before a public body and express themselves.

Also, you may be subjected to a time limit to present your case. If you bring enough people to the meeting and present your case in a reasonable and persuasive manner, you will make it difficult for the board to treat you with disrespect or to ignore completely the points you make.

In the final analysis, whether or not you can motivate the teacher, Head, Advisor, or Board of Governors to abandon an objectionable sex education programme will probably depend on your ability to convince whoever makes the decision that the programme is either severely deficient or else offensive to the sensibilities of a number of intelligent people.

It may be some consolation for you to know that a number of parents throughout the nation have been disturbed by the same kinds of materials and have been willing to voice their objections to teachers and other school authorities. While many have been disappointed in the response, more and more are reporting that they have been able to make significant changes both at the local and at the county levels. In fact, there are several national organisations that are deeply involved in the fight for decent and traditional approaches to sex education.

If you have problems that are not covered in this brief discussion, you may want to contact one or more of these groups. They will be happy to give you the benefit of their experience in supporting approaches to human sexuality that are more compatible with traditional family values.

10
Act For Change

A value-free, morally neutral, facts-only approach to sex education is counterproductive to solving the problems of pregnancy, abortion and disease among our teenagers. Certainly US statistics point consistently to the failure of such programmes to counteract the very problems they were set up to deal with. In spite of generous funding and publicity, teenage pregnancies, sexually transmitted diseases and abortions continue to rise where this approach is adopted; whereas abstinence-based sex education programmes are demonstrating a remarkable success in reducing teenage sexual activities and the attendant problems.

However, we must do more than teach reproduction and contraception if our kids are going to adopt a lifestyle of responsible moral behaviour. The outside pressure is too great. Peers, television, films, music and advertising constantly encourage kids to become sexually active. These negative influences often outweigh positive influences from other sources. Without consistent moral training from the school, church and home, our children will have a tough time incorporating positive values into their lives. Knowledge alone does not produce wisdom.

Needed—a united front

There was a time when the family, the church, the school
and the media provided a clear, consistent, unified message
to kids about morality. Parents teaching moral values at
home were supported on the other fronts. But today parents
often stand alone in the battle. The message promoted by
the powerful entertainment and advertising media suggests
that promiscuity is the rule and that the negative consequences from it are negligible. Surprisingly, even some
churches are going soft on the obvious positive moral
values. When the education system joins the campaign by
taking an alleged morally neutral position on sex education while failing properly to notify parents or involve
them in the process, we really feel like the rug is being
yanked out from under us.

Including parents and seeking their consent in matters of
morality are integral to effective sex education. School sex
education programmes would be more effective if parents
and their moral values were included in the planning.
Eunice Kennedy Shriver, Vice-president of the Kennedy
Foundation, says that the first step toward positive, healthy
sex education is to 'create a consistent, supportive network
of parents, teachers, doctors, nurses, clergy, friends and
counsellors who work with adolescents over an extended
period.' Parents also need to be included so the school programme can help them deal with sex-related issues at
home. Parents need the resources and support the school
can supply them for talking to their kids about sex.

Strong family relationships tend to discourage teenage
sexual activity. For example, studies show that a close
mother-daughter relationship reduces the likelihood of premarital sexual activity by the daughter. When sex education programmes take advantage of parental influence
instead of ignoring it, they are likely to be more successful.

Teach the consequences of promiscuity

The teenage sexuality crisis will never be resolved until our kids understand the devastating consequences of sexual promiscuity. Casual sex may be *safer* with condoms, but it is definitely not *safe*, contrary to what many family planning groups and sex educators imply. We must teach our kids about the life-threatening risks they take whenever they forego virginity and abstinence.

The phrases 'safe sex' and 'safer sex' can easily cause confusion. The advocates of comprehensive sex education coined the term 'safe sex' for encouraging condom use, and the universities sustained the false concept by sponsoring 'Safe Sex Week' programmes. Then, after strong opposition based on medical research into the failure rate of condoms and other methods of contraception, they changed the phrase to 'safer sex'. One can wonder how long it will be before they change that phrase to something else. Every year over half a million new cases of sexually transmitted diseases are treated at clinics in the UK.[23]

Teach moral values

Hopefully by now you will agree that sex education is neither value-free nor morally neutral. Even those programmes which claim to be such are promoting certain moral values (eg 'You're going to do it anyway, so wear a condom and protect yourself'; or, 'You're the only one who can decide what's best for you sexually'). Values are being communicated; the question is, what values or whose should be communicated? Should school-based sex education programmes continue to ignore traditional moral values of sexual behaviour while our kids stumble blindly through their relationships without a clue as to what's right and wrong?

Children have a psychological need to be taught positive values. Psychiatrist Melvin Anschell points out that 'today's children and adolescents need an educational system that upholds the family. . .a morality that supports the struggle for existence and sustains civilised life, rather than undermining it.'[24]

The US Department of Education issued a statement declaring that 'the surest way to prevent the spread of AIDS in the teenage and young adult population is for schools and parents to convey the reasons adolescents should be taught restraint in sexual activity. . . . The most important determinant of children's actions is their understanding of right and wrong.'

The cry for value-based, morally positive sex eduction is finding increasing support among nationally recognised authorities.

Dr Douglas Kirby summarises the reason for this consensus shift: 'When specific values were not clear goals of the course, there is much less evidence that sex education had any impact upon the students.'[25] We must return to teaching values because value-free sex education isn't working.

As a health teacher and educator, Coleen Mast correctly observes, 'Contraceptives are a poor substitute for the difficult and costly work of teaching adolescents to be responsible adults who can make moral distinctions. . . . How are adolescents to learn self-control, fidelity, responsibility and moral courage when so many adults fail to teach and model such qualities themselves?'[26]

Mast is very realistic when she observes, '(Adolescents) deserve moral support and encouragement because remaining chaste is not easy in the face of so many biological and cultural forces pressuring them to have sex. They need a sex education programme that will bring out the best in them'.

Based on all evidence presented, if we are sincerely concerned about reducing teenager promiscuity and pregnancy we should immediately and unashamedly return moral values to sex education curriculum, and rather than writing off institutions such as the church as outmoded, we should encourage the exploration of the moral and spiritual framework which seeks to uphold the dignity and self-restraint of young people.

Eliminate mixed messages about abstinence

A pregnancy prevention strategy must send a clear, consistent message about the acceptability or unacceptability of adolescent sexual behaviour. No pregnancy prevention programme can be expected to work if it sends a mixed message or if the surrounding culture undermines its message. Indeed, the effectiveness of any programme is largely dependent on the consistency of its message.

What is a mixed message? Margaret Whitehead, founder of the Educational Guidance Institute, says, 'Sex education programmes that say 'Don't have sex; but if you do, use a contraceptive' are conveying a double message that undercuts the desired message about sexual abstinence.'[27]

The mixed message, which is really a recommendation for contraception, harms teenagers both physically and emotionally. First, due to the statistical failure rate of all contraceptives except abstinence, the mixed message can result in physical complications that teenagers didn't bargain for: pregnancy, cervical cancer, abortion, unwanted birth or sexually transmitted disease.

Second, the mixed message almost always results in emotional starvation. Kids need to escape their loneliness and find acceptance and security through love, but too often these needs are confused with what the surrounding culture presents as the 'need' for sex. Even when kids are successful at the game of sexual roulette (they have sex and beat the odds against pregnancy and STDs), they still come away from the encounter with their needs unmet.

Other psychological and emotional consequences of premarital sex can be equally serious. These include feelings of guilt, fear, self-hatred, doubt, disappointment, the pain of exploiting or being exploited by another person, and the stunting of growth in personal identity and social relationships. Teenagers may be successful at preventing pregnancy during promiscuity, but there's no such things as a condom for the mind and the heart which are always vulnerable to great injury when the message about premarital sex is unclear.

Many teenagers are surprised and sobered to learn that contraceptives also offer no protection against the powerful emotional bonding that takes place during sexual intercourse. The sensations and emotions that intercourse stimulates leave a deep impression on the memory. A person retains memories of the sex partner, the circumstances and the emotions long after intercourse has taken place and the relationship has dissolved.

Adolescents need a set of guidelines that will help them discover who they are and help them form healthy relationships. 'Be careful!' is not enough, nor is it enough to tell teenagers that premarital sex is acceptable if they are 'ready' or 'responsible,' or if they 'think through' their decision before taking action. We must not assume that an adolescent understands these concepts in the same way an adult would. We must instead provide information and directions that can be understood on the concrete level of reasoning.

Implement abstinence-based programmes

The parents, educators and school governors who are

unhappy with the philosophy and results of so-called value-free, morally neutral sex education in schools have two possible alternatives. The first is to eliminate sex education from the state school system.

However, adolescents benefit from receiving at least some of their sex education in school. Teenagers characteristically test and evaluate in the outside world principles they have learned inside the home. They need to verify what their parents have taught them about truth and morality by checking it against what they hear from other authority figures, particularly teachers. Therefore the second alternative is to keep sex education in the schools, but to change the content from value-free to value-based.

If sex education in the classroom presents positive moral values which promote physical, emotional and spiritual well-being, the school becomes an important ally to parents by reinforcing what many teenagers have already learned at home. Teenagers will be doubly equipped to make the decisions that will help them build moral character now and establish sound families of their own in the future. Those students whose home situation is morally negative in teaching and/or example will benefit even more from a value-based state school sex education curriculum.

Where does a concerned, involved parent, educator or school governor begin? What kinds of questions must you ask in order to determine the appropriateness of an abstinence-based sex education course for school use? Dr Dinah Richard, who consults with schools and parent organisations on abstinence-based programmes, provides a 30-question checklist for evaluating sex education programmes and materials:

1. Are parents included in the school's process of setting policies and guidelines and of selecting materials?
2. Does the programme have tangible means of direct

parental involvement other than the negative means of simply opting to have their children taken out of the class?

3. Are parents presented respectfully, as a valuable resource, as persons to turn to for help and as persons with whom to discuss sensitive issues?

4. Does the programme have a moral perspective that teaches what is right and wrong, directing students toward the right choices?

5. Does the programme use correct, not slang, terminology?

6. Does it teach that the sex drive is controllable and that abstinence is realistic?

7. Does it define abstinence as restraint from all sexual activity, not simply one form of intercourse?

8. Does the programme use the phrase 'premarital abstinence' rather than terms such as 'postponing' or 'delaying' sex (or premarital sex)?

9. Is abstinence presented as positive behaviour and premarital sex as destructive behaviour?

10. Does the programme refute the myth that 'everybody is doing it'?

11. Does the programme promote secondary virginity?

12. Does the programme teach the techniques of saying no?

13. Does the programme present the tragic physical and emotional consequences of premarital sex?

14. Is the programme free of double messages? Does the programme omit a discussion or demonstration of contraceptive devices?

15. Does the programme refute the notion of 'safe sex,' telling students about contraceptive failures?

16. When questions about alternative lifestyle or deviant behaviours are brought up, does the instructor refrain from discussion, referring students to their parents for

information instead?

17. Is the latency period (elementary school age) protected?

18. Do materials avoid sexually explicit content?

19. Is the word 'marriage' used rather than 'monogamous relationship?'

20. Is marriage presented as a legal, moral and spiritual commitment?

21. Is sex presented as a favourable and enjoyable act occurring within marriage for unitive and procreative purposes?

22. Are love, fidelity, and commitment presented as standards within marriage?

23. Is the family defined as a blood or legal relationship?

24. Is pregnancy presented as an exciting event within a marriage?

25. Is the family presented as a source of love, nurturing and stability?

26. Does the programme respect the student's privacy and the family's privacy?

27. Do materials and films use positive role models instead of pop stars?

28. Is the teacher an appropriate role model?

29. Are students asked to portray or write about only wholesome topics?

30. Are all materials age-appropriate?

Conclusion

Teenage promiscuity, pregnancies, abortions and out-of-wedlock births are all on an unprecedented increase. This is doubly alarming in the light of massive government programmes aimed at reducing these rates. The fundamental flaw is apparent, the evidence overwhelming: 'value free' sex education, by operating under false assumptions about teenage sexuality and by proposing unrealistic solutions, has failed in its task.

Without moralising or sermonising, it is time for those who work with teenagers and who are concerned about their future well-being—teachers, youth workers, parents and school governors—to promote a positive alternative that will reverse the current destructive trends and advocate not 'safer sex' but fulfilled sex in the context of loving, committed marriage.

Notes

1. Gordon, Sol, and Everly, Kathleen. 'Increasing Self-Esteem in Vulnerable Students. . .A Tool for Reducing Pregnancy Among Teenagers.' Reprinted from *Impact* '85, 2:Article 41:9-17. Publication of Institute for Family Research and Education, 760 Ostrom Avenue, Syracuse, NY 13210-2999.

2. Klucoff, Carol. 'Teens: Speaking Their Minds.' *Washington Post*, 3rd February 1982.

3. Morgan, Anne Marie. 'Comprehensive Sex Education: Ten Fatal Flaws.' Virginians for Family Values.

4. Mosbacker, Barrett. 'Teen Pregnancy and School-Based Health Clinics.' *Vision*, October/November 1986.

5. See Note 4.

6. Richard, Dinah. 'Exemplary abstinence-based sex education programs.' *The World & I*. A publication of The Washington Times Corporation, © September 1989.

7. Ravenel, S. DuBose, MD. 'Birth Control Doesn't Curb

Teen Pregnancies.' *News and Observer* (Raleigh, NC, 28th June 1989).

8. McIlhaney, Joe S., MD. *CMS Journal* XVIII:1 (Winter 1987).

9. 'American Teens Speak: Sex, Myth, TV and Birth Control.' The Planned Parenthood Poll. Louise Harris and Associates, Inc, September/October 1986.

10. 'Legalised Abortion and the Public Health'. Report of a study by the Institute of Medicine, National, Academy of Sciences, Washington DC, May 1975.

11. Written testimony of Faye Wattleton before Jeremiah Denton. Title XX Hearings, 31st March 1981.

12. Speckhard, Anne Catherine. 'The Psycho-Social Aspects of Stress Following Abortion.' A thesis submitted to the Faculty of the Graduate School of the University of Minnesota, May 1985.

13. 'Legalised Abortion and the Public Health.' Washington DC: The Institute of Medicine, National Academy of Sciences, May 1975.

14. 'Teenage Pregnancy: The Problem That Hasn't Gone Away.' From a report on a study done by the Alan Guttmacher Institute, Section 5, New York, 1981.

15. Hall, C., and Zisook, S. 'Psychological Distress Following Therapeutic Abortion.' *The Female Patient* 8 (March 1983).

16. Kumar, R., and Robson, K. *Psychological Medicine* 8 (1978).

17. Bulfin, M., MD. 'A New Problem in Adolescent Gynecology.' *Southern Medical Journal* 72:8 (August 1979).

18. See Note 17.

19. 'Sexual Addiction Can Lead to Destruction.' *USA Today*, 2nd February 1989.

20. See Note 19.

21. *Insider*. A PPFA publication, May 1988.

22. Whelan, Dr Elizabeth. *Sex and Sensibility: A New Look at Being a Woman*. New York: McGraw-Hill Book Co, 1974.

23. *19* Magazine, March 1992.

24. Anchell, Melvin, MD. *Sex and Insanity*. Portland, Oregon; Halcyon House, 1983.

25. Kirby, Douglas. *Sexuality Education: An Evaluation of Programs and Their Effects*. Santa Cruz, CA: Network Publication, 1984.

26. Mast, Coleen. 'Sex and Sanctity of Love – Beyond Biology.' *The World & I*. A publication of The Washington Times Corporation, © September 1989. Used by permission.

27. Bauer, Ed. 'Sex Education Program Must Have a Clear and Consistent Message.' *Bulletin*. Albermarle County, Virginia, 15th March 1988.

Resources

Stammers, Dr Trevor. *The Family Guide to Sex and Intimacy* (Hodder and Stoughton).

Sexual Relationships and Marriage, CARE Family Booklets, Number 1.

Sex is Not a Four Letter Word (Scripture Press).

Moon, Phil. *Hanging in There* (Monarch Publications/CPAS).

Dixon, Dr Patrick. *The Truth About AIDS* (Kingsway Publications).

Houghton, John and Janet. *Parenting Teenagers* (Kingsway Publications).

Houghton, John and Janet. *A Touch of Love* (Kingsway Publications).

For further advice and information on resources available, contact the Christian Initiative on Teenage Sexuality, Care for the Family, 136 Newport Road, Cardiff CF2 1DJ (Telephone 0222 494431).